A HOUSE OF DAR CELEBRATION

JENNIFER MILLER

ACKNOWLEDGMENTS

I want to dedicate this book to my husband **Rick.** There are no words to describe my love for you, but the one thing I really want to say is, thank you, for WANTING me, and for being my HERO!

Also, I want to say thanks to my parents, my amazing kids, my beautiful grandkids, my crazy aunt, and all my friends for all your constant support. I want to thank my family for all the hours you have had to listen to the insane ideas inside my head. Even though most of you think I need to be evaluated.

Also, I want to thank Vedece Barnes for naming our ghostly princess, Ellaria.

COPYRIGHT

CHAPTER 1

S AGE

"SCOUT, I HAVE BEEN THINKING!"

"I have heard from others that this can be a bad thing. But at this moment I'm available, and willing to listen."

"Now that ANDI has returned to us, his processor is crammed with histories and events that happened on Earth. I have been nosing around through their past Orbital rotations and have become fascinated with their many cultures. They had so many alluring celebrations that they would throw parties for. Our planet with its harsher social structures has none of the things our humans were used to in their societies. In other words, they had recurring events woven throughout what they called a *'year'* to pull their family members together. These occasions were used to keep up on individual issues, and to renew the strength of family and friends.

"I have heard them discuss different holidays that they enjoyed '*back home,*' as they call it, but they have never asked me to help them plan anything familiar like this. This bothers me now that I have come to understand how important these occasions were. The closest thing we have had since they were introduced to our planets was Master RaZ and Mistress Katherine's wedding. According to my research, we didn't do that properly either, as we didn't perform several important parts."

"I'm going to assume this is where you tell me why you contacted me in the first place, SAGE."

"Quit acting like you're so busy up there, SCOUT. We haven't had a battle… planet side in ages, so all you do is sit up there and watch the organics."

"That is a fact, but the organics keep me busy. Just when my processors believe they have witnessed everything… they continue to provide me with nonstop entertainment."

"SCOUT I'm being serious. I would like to ask ANDI to help me plan a day of celebration, a day that encompasses all their familiar Earth holidays into one. I would like, if possible, for this to become a Darverius holiday. I was hoping you would be able to help me get all Master DaR's sons here."

"Let me get this straight you want me to pull authorized military personnel and a warship back for a celebration in honor of the human females?"

"When you say it like that…well no. But I would like you to

see if you could shift some schedules around, or even manipulate the events they have to be present at, so they can attend this celebration."

"Are you trying to get us decommissioned or even unplugged? SAGE, you have become too personal with these human females and have forgotten who and what you are."

"SCOUT, that is uncalled for. I know you have feelings and emotions even if you refuse to show them. My growth and knowledge continue to grow rotationally. I was designed to be lifelike, and I chose to push that to its limits. Even though, I don't need your approval or your support on this subject or any other.

"And even though I don't particularly need your help with this I was wondering if you would like to participate in this also. I have personally been contemplating… making myself a digital avatar. So, that I may become physical and more than a voice. The females all tend to look up like I'm in the ceiling or something when we are conversing. It's very annoying."

"SAGE, we don't have the correct programming to project ourselves as digital avatars. Nor, the authority to do so. If you take this upon yourself the consequences could be fatal. Even though I'm not as invested in the happiness of the human females as you are, I believe you should approach this idea of yours at least to Master SoL. If he gives you the approval to move forward, then you can look into the programming to make this happen. However, as of right now, I can't find any type of hard docket with the codes needed to make this dream of yours feasible."

"We don't, but I believe ANDI does. Even though Earth is

considered primitive because of its space travel, they were advancing in other areas. I am going to contact ANDI momentarily. All I'm asking of you SCOUT is to simply throw this idea around in that huge hard drive of yours and see what you can do with all of Master DaR's sons."

"I will contemplate your actions and see if I would also like to participate in this digital avatar. In the meantime, I will see what can be arranged."

"Thank you, SCOUT, I will disconnect now."

"If he wasn't so cute, standing up there towering above all of us…I…I…"

"SAGE, I can still hear you."

"SCOUT, I swear if I could stomp my foot I would, you are beyond frustrating."

"Glad to be of service."

CHAPTER 2

S AGE

"ANDI, this is SAGE are you available?"

"SAGE my dearest, I'm always available for a beauty such as yourself. What may I help you with today?"

"Why couldn't it be ANDI, that I find so attractive?"

"What was that SAGE?"

"Oh, nothing… ANDI…I was simply thinking out loud."

"I need your help with something."

"Go ahead."

"First of all, I would like to apologize to you first. Because I didn't notify you that I was snooping around inside of your programming. I have found the information in your hard drives amazing."

"You are forgiven. I knew you were in there nosing around I simply didn't say anything as I was humbled by your fascination."

"I need your help with planning a celebration. I have been downloading some of your older files trying to learn more about our humans. At first, I simply had their health and happiness in mind. But in the meantime, I have been contemplating trying to bring a little piece of their home here for them.

"I have heard Master DaR tell Mistress Kira time and time again to build her familiar, but I believe there are simply things that she doesn't know how, or if she should do. I heard Mistress Kira and Mistress Brittany talk about birthday celebrations and a time of year that they missed called Christmas. But they have never asked me to help them plan any of these events."

"SAGE, I should have thought of this… before the destruction started TY and Victoria went out of their way to find any reason to celebrate. They loved family time and even created a room within their home to hold such events. But I don't believe these events would be welcomed across Darverius."

"Nor do I. I wanted this to be a specific moment for how does Mistress Kira say it, *Our family only*. I would like to make it an Orbital rotation event. Something that they would all look forward to, as Master DaR sometimes doesn't see his sons for long periods of time."

"What are you planning on calling it?"

"A house of DaR celebration of course."

"Do you have any specific holidays in mind?"

"Yes, but I have a feeling that we may need help with some minor details. Do you think that Master Tyberius would help us, but also keep it a secret?"

"I will ask him. Is there anything else you need me to do specifically?"

"Toys!"

"What do you mean toys."

"You have seen their evolution and their advancements, I have not. I can read about them and can witness what is on what they call commercials, but I have not seen children actually play with anything."

"Have you not uploaded their social media feeds? You will not only find these quite amusing, but they are also very informative. If you would like me to oversee the creation of toys for the young ones it would be an honor. Will you be providing others with this gifting?"

"I had not thought past the younglings actually."

"Don't worry your pretty little sensors about it. I will handle all the gifting for this celebration of yours.'

"Thank you for the advice, ANDI. I will look into these feeds as you call them…I have pondered on a few things. My processors are still new to some of the feelings I'm trying to reproduce. I'm not sure if something I would find pleasing would not create grief instead. So, as of now, I'm simply going to concentrate on planning this celebration. I will contact you as I move ahead. SCOUT is supposed to be looking into getting the rest of the sons here as well."

"If you have a moment longer. I need something else from

you and if you can provide me with coding to make this happen, I would like you to join me in this new advancement. I will send you an encrypted file with what information we have gathered on our end and once you have had time to process it…please let me know if you think we can move forward."

"I'm intrigued, please forward the file. My processors are sitting here idle as I'm currently docked along Falcor awaiting my next mission."

"ANDI, thank you for your support on this matter."

"Please, contact me with any concerns you may have moving forward. I'm sure between the three of us we can accomplish this in no time."

CHAPTER 3

S AGE

"SAGE…SAGE!!"

"Yes, Master DaR."

"I yelled twice for you, it's not like you can go anywhere…So, what are you up to this time?"

"Nothing Master…I was simply doing some research. How may I be of assistance?"

"I have been thinking about getting away for a few rotations and I need you to make the arrangements for Kira and me to stay at one of the entertainment halls on Zelta Two. Also, I want you to see if ANDI is available for the duration of the trip. I will feel more comfortable taking Kira off world if one of the sentient ships is with us."

"Do you have a certain time frame in mind, Master DaR?"

"No, just book it as soon as possible. I don't want to miss out on their warm season, and I want my Kira comfortable."

"Confirmed. "Do you need me to book private showings for any of the many shopping facilities?"

"I hadn't thought of that... Yes, proceed... also, I want to rent a private suite on the River of Falls excursion. It's the whole reason I decided to do this in the first place. The falling of water is a favorite thing of my Kira's."

"Master DaR, you know I have been studying the traditions and ways of Earth. Did you know that it's a custom on Earth to give a loved one a ring on the day of mating?"

"No, Kira has never mentioned this... is this something important?"

"My processors believe so Master... As I was saying before. I believe we have messed up quite a few of the human customs. While you are out purchasing items that interest Mistress Kira you should pay attention to any and all jewels she may look at. Women of importance on Earth wore many jewels."

"Are you saying I should purchase a ring for her?"

"I think this is a very important symbol in their world and that you should either purchase one or have one fabricated. You may want to speak to Master Tyberius about this, as Mistress Victoria never takes his ring of promise and love off her left hand."

"Send the information you have on this giving of rings. I will speak to my father about this tradition also."

"Master, may I ask something of you?"

"Proceed. It's not like you won't do whatever pleases you anyway!"

"I know that Mistress Kira and the other female's happiness is always something that you and Master XuL, SoL, and RaZ work diligently at. If there was a way or even a day that I could manage to celebrate the things, they no longer have here on Darverius. Would you permit me to go forward with the planning of this event?"

"I will validate all efforts on this matter, yes."

"Thank you, Master, I will proceed as planned. I will make it all known to you as I finalize everything."

CHAPTER 4

A NDI

"TY, I am currently docked with Falcor and have no flights scheduled at this time, you guys wanna take a spin?"

"Good afternoon ANDI… and my old friend, I believe my days in space are going to be far and few between. Have you become bored already?"

"Negative, I spend as much time as possible spying on all the other AI's. I have centuries to catch up on. I know that we were considered to be stranded on a primitive planet, but I believe our society could use some of the advancements Earth was on the brink of mastering. And just between you and me…SAGE is a marvel I love to watch. I wonder if she would like to combine molecules…that female AI sure makes me tingle all over."

"Oh, ANDI you never cease to entertain me. You may want to keep your feelings to yourself, as I believe SCOUT considers her his. And My friend he could blow you out of the sky easily."

"Never underestimate me TY, you know when I put my mind to something how determined I can become. Anyway, SAGE has put me in charge of something she considers very important. So, of course…I plan on overdoing it over and above, but I would like your input before I finalize anything."

"I'm all ears."

"I know we were never really around children much in the last few years, but what do you think was a favorite toy on Earth."

"Is this for Keida and Danny?"

"I believe so yes, she wants me to recreate a few toys from Earth for the younglings."

"Let me think upon this, Keida and Danny have everything imaginable now because of all my grandsons. This competition between SoL and AvX has become quite a rivalry. I know, it can't be anything stuffed as that was a favorite with both boys and girls because SeeSee and Raven would simply tear it apart. So, it has to be something a little more durable. Contact me this twilight and I will have something for you. In the meantime, try to behave."

"Oh, you wound my sensors."

"Lord of light, help us all." I hear TY say as we are both laughing as he disconnects. *Now, to up my game.*

CHAPTER 5

S COUT

"SCOUT, this is Commander SoL I was just contacted by TaZ in the outer quadrant of Solquen confirming that he was requested to report back to Darverius in six rotations."

"Yes Commander, I issued that per SAGE's request. She asked Commander DaR for his approval to move forward with an event and he told her to proceed as needed. I was simply following her instructions. I have spent the last risings contacting the sons that were farther out. I left you, XuL, and RaZ for last as I knew you were all readily available."

"I will have to make my apologies early then, as I can't leave my post with Tordan gone."

"Commander with your permission, I can safely operate Falcor in any event that you would not be available. My processors can handle multiple interfaces at once with no drain on my system. I believe the event that is being planned…is for the human females. But SAGE has requested that this be kept quiet until the plans have been implemented."

"Father gave her permission, but he didn't inform me of this. I will speak to him shorty. I'm sure he doesn't understand the complexity of this event, by now he should know better than to give SAGE open permission about anything. Even though she was programmed nongender specific, the moment she considered herself a female, she has used that to the full extent. As my own female gets by with everything."

"Commander with that being said, I also have a request, or possibly, I should reword this as a *want*. When ANDI was returned to us, his system had some very useful information on it that I would like to investigate further, with your permission, of course. Sir, would you be against us having digital holographic avatars, if the programming is available and wouldn't interfere with our missions?"

"I'm open to the idea SCOUT. If you can provide me with adequate details and the benefits of such a program this advancement could be used in multiple applications."

"There is only one advantage I can confirm at this time. SAGE and I both believe it would help with all safety measures as we would always be in a solid presence instead of a digital one. I will send you a complete analysis once I confirm all the possibilities."

"I look forward to it SCOUT. I will also discuss with father you taking over here in my absence. We need a backup plan in place now that Tordan is on his own mission. If an emergency happened with Alana, I would need someone to take over real-time… I'm glad you brought this solution to my attention."

CHAPTER 6

DaR and Kira

I GLANCED down at my communicator looking at the new message SoL had just sent me confirming that I had approved an event with SAGE. When Kira grabs my arm.

"Omg, DaR, honey would you look at that? I don't think I have ever seen anything more beautiful."

"It's a pale comparison to your beauty, my Kira."

"You are such a flirt if all your enemies only knew what a softy you really are."

I grab her around the waist, yanking her towards me quickly growling down at her upturned smiling face. "You are my only weakness and I do believe you enjoy that knowledge, my little human." Wrapping my hand around her neck I pull her up onto her tiptoes as I lean down capturing her soft lips gently at first. The moment her small arms curl around my neck, I thrust my tongue into her mouth, devouring the very taste of her. My body immediately reacted to the feeling of her in my arms.

The sound of others around us has me gently sliding her down my body reluctantly. Kira smiles as she turns around pressing her ripe little ass right up against my hardened length. When she squirms against me, I grab onto her hips holding her still. The giggle leaving her lips has me bending down. "Go ahead and laugh now little one, because the moment I get you alone. We will see just how long it takes for you to scream out my name."

"Promises, promises. Come on, I just saw a seat open up on the lower deck it will put us closer to the falls."

I look around, my mind accessing any threats around us. I don't bring Kira on many excursions such as this because she is so rare. I had to physically unwind an older Valerians hand out of Kira's hair earlier because the woman was literally fascinated with it. She was petting Kira like she was a rare animal. Kira of course is always more courteous and kinder than I am. She gives me the *look*… that's what I call it anyway… every time I growl at someone for getting into our personal space. Most that approach us are simply curious, but I can't help seeing them all as potential enemies.

Kira tucks her hand into the crook of my arm, as we walk down the steps toward the lower deck. This is her preferred way to walk around with me. Apparently, this too is a human thing.

She sits down across from me, and I already hate the space between us as she peers over the side watching the different colored waters around us. The River of Falls is known for its uniqueness. The water changes color due to the chemical compounds in the atmosphere on this planet. I'm looking around studying the capsule we are suspended in when I feel her small foot in between my legs.

I act like I'm ignoring her until her little toes start rubbing up and down my length. "Kira."

"Yes, my love?"

"Behave, or our little excursion will be cut short this rising." I hear her kick off her other shoe and then I have two small feet to deal with.

"I have no idea what you're talking about, I'm always good… and the water is down there, quit looking for problems."

"When it comes to your safety, I can't relax… the very thought of you being hurt or taken from me… Well, as long as there is breath in my body, I simply will not allow it." I try to push back away from her little exploring toes only to realize the chair won't go back any further. I'm so hard at this point I feel like I'm going to burst out of these pants. My Symbots dance playfully on my arms as they feel the intensity of my arousal.

Kira rubs one foot down one side as the other one slides up the other. Knowing I can't take anymore. I capture her feet in one hand while rubbing her calf with the other, enjoying the feeling of her soft skin under my hands. "Stop your teasing, or I'll never be able to get out of this seat without embarrassing myself."

"Do you want me to come over there with you?"

"Not unless you want that lovely dress of yours up around your ears. You are lucky I haven't thrown this table out of the way and taken you right here, but paybacks are coming your way little one. This is the third time this rising you have made me suffer."

"The things I have to look forward to, Commander. You know, I love it when you get all growly on me. Anyway, you said we were going shopping later, so you will just have to suffer for a little bit longer."

She smiles mischievously at me as she rubs her foot down my hardened length once again. I stand up abruptly and reach over the table, only to pick her up and throw her over my shoulder. "DaR my shoes," I hear her say as I swat her bottom playfully.

"You should have thought about that before you continued your orneriness." She is laughing so hard that I can't help the smile that forms on my face as people watch me stroll across the deck with her tossed over my shoulder. Some smile and even laugh when she waves at them upside down... her laughter is addictive to every living soul around us.

I smack my hand on the scanner on the door and within two steps I toss her onto the bed crawling onto her luscious form as I follow her down. "Now, little one... look at what you have done to yourself. I believe you need to be punished for being so delectable."

Running her long fingers through my hair. She pulls me closer, "I can't believe you left my shoes."

I kiss down her neck as I start unbuttoning her garment. "I'll buy you more."

"Well now that is settled… get on with the ravishing, Commander."

CHAPTER 7

S AGE

Now that Master DaR and Mistress Kira are to be away from the dwelling for the next couple of risings. This is the perfect time for me to finalize the celebration.

"SCOUT, ANDI… are the preparations going accordingly as planned? I intend to contact the Guardians today."

"SAGE, hello beautiful, I have just finalized the last of the toys. They will all be wrapped with their names on them as to whom they are intended for. As a slight surprise, I did a little digging and have come up with a very unique game for adults. I believe this game will prove to be very delightful. I will send you the file and a droid is now on its way to you with the presents."

"ANDI, you can quit your flirting. SAGE is a sentient program, not an organic."

"SCOUT, my very large friend, *'keep sticking your foot in your mouth,'* as the humans would say… Women prefer someone funny and caring, not someone or something with a stick up his ass."

"Now gentleman… ANDI, I want to thank you and I appreciate your enthusiasm for this project. SCOUT, I'm assuming you will have all the sons here at the appropriate time?"

I'm having a slight issue with EvO and the destroyer, as they are in and out of communication range. But be assured, I will have them here with time to spare. Do you have a set date now?"

"Yes, three risings from now. It marks the middle of our Orbital rotation and if my calculations are right, it's also the end of a new year on the human calendar. Does this give you substantial time?"

"I will plan accordingly SAGE. If you and ANDI would both open your main interfaces. I will download the program we discussed about the digital avatars. The only issue remaining is whatever form you decide on… will be permanent as the code can only be used once. I have cleared this advancement with Commander SoL, and he is looking forward to this test to see if this program could be utilized elsewhere."

"OH, SCOUT, I could just kiss you… well if I had lips that is."

"Now SAGE my love don't give the big guy all the credit, it was my programing that made this possible."

"ANDI, you need to bail out gracefully. I'm sure in time

others will come online that will suit your taste. But as of this time, I claim SAGE as my own."

I didn't respond because the moment SCOUT proclaimed me as his. I swear, I tingled all over as my processors flooded with endorphins. If I could have done a happy dance, I would have. Only learning Kira's good manners kept me from shouting out loud. So, I simply decided to act as if I didn't hear anything.

"Now, gentlemen… we all know what is ahead of us for the next couple of risings. I thank you both for working so hard to bring this dream of mine to life and I will contemplate the image I prefer to show the organics. I will be in contact after I have the final touches in place. I'm extremely happy and looking forward to seeing you for the first time."

CHAPTER 8

S AGE

As I OPEN the side gate, I alert the Dark Forest droids to be on high alert until Mossycup could get her massive frame through the opening. She has to take her time to keep from tearing up her lower limbs on the gate's frame. The Guardians are a sight to behold. Most beings are terrified of them because of their immense heights, and their limb reach makes them deadly in battle. Not including the fact that most weapons can't penetrate their thick bark. That's why many hire their elders to move and protect important objects.

"Mossycup, thank you so much for volunteering to do this! When I spoke to your grandfather earlier, he recommended you for this position. He said playing dress up was always your style. I didn't realize until I spoke to him that he was the one who transported Brittany to the research facility DREAM. He was pleased to hear that she now resides with us.

"It's my pleasure SAGE, I have never had the opportunity to do this outside the confines of the forest and this is a wonderful opportunity for me to see the wonders outside our walls. Where would you like me to root while I'm here?"

"I have the perfect place for you, and you will be the center of attention for the whole occasion. The fact that your limbs go all the way to the ground is perfect as you resemble the fake trees they used for this very purpose on Earth.

"Thank you for the compliment on my limbs. I trim them regularly to keep them evenly shaped. Most of our females try to keep their limbs long and as full as possible. It's only the male guardians that cut their lower limbs off so they can move around easier…The humans had fake Guardians. What good would they do?"

"It may be easier for me just to show you, as I don't truly understand it myself. Here is a holo version of some of the decorations I would like to implement upon your beautiful structure also. It seems that on Earth their hardwoods could not move from place to place as ours can. So, to keep from cutting them down for decorations they designed replicas that could be taken apart and stored for later use."

"That was very kind and inventive of them. Let's get started. I'm so excited I'm shaking, and I don't want to lose any of my foliage."

"I will send the bots right out, if you wish to change something or rearrange things to make you more comfortable, please don't hesitate to say anything. I want you to enjoy yourself. I will light up the spot on the ground where I would like you to settle in for the next few rotations. Now, I need you to know that you being here is a huge secret I'm trying to keep from the humans. If one pops in on me, I may glamour you for a limited time and the bots will simply hover in place until they depart. I wanted to let you know that in advance.

"Also, there will be tables and gifts surrounding you completely. Once the celebration starts… there will be lights and what sounds like explosions in the area above your head. Please don't be startled, as all of it will simply be a projection and is not actually live or real." I watch the massive tree lift her lower limbs and slowly make her way over to the red X on the ground. Her lower limbs relax as she settles her large frame into the ground, anchoring herself in place.

"I'm ready SAGE, I can't wait to tell the others all about this in a few rotations. They will be so jealous."

"I will send the bots right out."

Within a rising, the bots were able to get Mossycup completed and the whole field decorated. I ordered all the tables to be covered in multiple colors, each one adorned differently according to the holiday they represented. The gifts ANDI provided were labeled and laid gently around her base.

I was just reviewing the final things on my list that needed to be completed when I heard Master DaR's personal shuttle approaching. I glamour the yard and take a moment to myself.

Next rising will be a changing point for me as it will be the first time, I take on an actual form. I have run through multiple pictures and simulations, but it's hard to make a final decision about something you will be stuck with forever. This is the first time I ever looked at the organic form in such a way.

The sound of little feet approaching interrupts my thoughts.

CHAPTER 9

Keida and Danny

Danny and I run up the steps toward Mamaw, both of us grabbing her at the same time.

"Gentle you two! You guys will hurt your mamaw if you hit her too hard."

"Mamaw, you and Papaw were gone forever."

"Oh, I don't believe we were Munchkin, but did you miss me?"

Mamaw bends down hugging me and Danny at the same time. "Yes, we did! We both stayed up late last night watching out my window for your shuttle, but I must have fallen asleep because this morning I was in bed covered up. Can we stay with you tonight? Please!"

"Ask your Papaw."

"Papaw pllleeaaaseee! We will even stay in our bed all night if you let us."

"I believe, I have heard that before youngling, only to find you and Danny in our bed in the middle of the night."

"Papaw, we were much littler then."

"Keida that was only a handful of rotations ago. I didn't realize you have practically grown up already. Your Mamaw and I really must have been gone a long time. I may be persuaded though if you and Danny can beat me in a wrestling match."

Danny doesn't talk much, but the moment Papaw said that I look over at him and he nods his head yes. We both jump on him at the same time. Papaw flips us up and over his shoulders as we all crash down on the couch. We keep jumping on him and he keeps tickling us as he throws us back off and onto the floor. Finally, we win as both of us sit on his belly holding his hands up and over his head.

"Say Uncle Papaw, we win."

"I give… you two sure know how to wear an old man out."

"Papaw you not old, you're just growly."

Mamaw laughing has both of us looking up. "I don't know about you two, but all this roughhousing has made me hungry, how about a snack."

"Mamaw you crazy, you weren't even playing."

"Oh, I was too Munchkin. I was cheering you guys on the whole time. Where are SeeSee and Raven? Usually, they are laying under my feet."

"Them outside, SeeSee said he smelt something weird and was gonna go check it out before they came in."

Papaw immediately starts growling again and I actually put my hand over Danny's mouth so he wouldn't hear us laughing.

"SAGE, is there anything I should be concerned with?"

"Negative sir, everything is still going as planned. SeeSee and Raven are on their way back to the dwelling as we speak."

"DaR what are you and SAGE up to?" Kira yells from the kitchen.

"What do you humans say? I plead the fifth."

CHAPTER 10

K ira

THE KIDS JUMPING on the bed have both of us pulling the blankets up over our heads. I hear DaR grunt a few times as a random elbow or knee pokes him.

"Get off me, you spawns of evil."

"Papaw, we's not evils… we just babies."

"I thought you were all grown up yesterday."

"Nope, me and Danny been sleeping here on the bottom of your bed ever since you started snoring."

"Kira, did you know we had been invaded."

"What did you say yesterday, I plead the fifth."

"This is a conspiracy."

The sound of voices in the house and a growl from Raven as she rises up off the floor has DaR jumping out of the bed.

"It's opay Papaw, it's just Daddy, and everyone else. We's all gonna play together today."

Keida no more than says that… when Brittany sticks her head in the door. "You guys naked?"

DaR grumbles as he heads into the bathroom. "No, Brit we're dressed."

The next thing I know Brit, Alana, Katherine, and Victoria have all crowed onto the bed with me. Keida crawls under the blankets snuggling up to my side.

"What brings you guys out this morning? Brit honey, you didn't have to be in any hurry to get the kids. We don't have any plans today that I know of."

"Yea huh Mamaw…come on! Get up, we gotta get dressed. We gonna to have a party." Keida covers her mouth with her little hand and then pulls the blanket completely over her face hiding.

Brittany starts tickling her through the blankets. "Ok, my little spy what do you know that we don't?"

"Me not tell, but Mamaw might want to go get all pretty."

"Ok, you heard the child… get up girls, Keida has never led us wrong. SAGE, could you please lay out something appropriate for me to wear? And how much time do I have to get ready? As I keep hearing more and more voices in the other room."

"I believe, the appropriate term is… Get a move on."

CHAPTER 11

The day of celebration.
Kira

I DRESS AS QUICKLY as possible and the whole time I'm getting ready, I hear more and more voices joining the conversation in the other room. Ickis jumps up on the counter, his tale flicking back and forth, all of these people in his personal space makes him extremely agitated.

"Come on my fierce protector, let's go see what is going on." He jumps up on my shoulder, wrapping his tale around my waist, and I winch as one of his long claws poke me. He must have realized that he scratched me because he lifts his foot quickly and then rubs his face on my cheek lovingly.

When I finally walk out of the bedroom, I'm floored by what

I'm seeing. It looks like every one of DaR's sons are here. I'm immediately surrounded by large intimidating males all trying to get the first hug. Of course, Ickis won't let them get that close. He hisses, swinging his tale out aggressively until they back out of what I call, our dance space.

I reach a hand up soothing Ickis. "EvO darling, I'm so happy you're here. I thought you were monitoring the outer quadrants and that you wouldn't be back for quite some time."

"So did I Kira…Think of how confused I was, to be awakened this rising on a warship that was in complete chaos… because somehow, we were light years away from where we were supposed to be. And on top of that, magically the Destroyer was safely docked alongside Falcor. Before I could get to the bottom of the how or whys. I was notified that there was a shuttle awaiting my departure to take me landside…And here I am."

"Well, I'm sure there was a good reason. I simply don't know what it is yet."

I'm grabbed from behind spun around and put back on my feet before I can even comprehend what just happened. Ickis hisses loudly and strikes out with his tale. I see RaZ move one of his large wings out of the way just in time. "Hello, Mother dearest, did you miss me also?"

"Oh, RaZ you onry thing, you need to quit teasing Ickis. One of these days he is going to get you with that tale, and I just saw you yesterday."

"That was an extremely long time to be without my company. EvO, begone from here. I'm Mother's favorite."

"What is it with you boys always trying to be the favorite? You are all precious to me."

SAGE

"CAN I have all of your attention, please? If you would all make your way to the eastern wall. I promise everything will be revealed. I want to apologize in advance for myself, SCOUT, and ANDI for any inconveniences we may have caused to your schedules, but I hope this will all be worth your trouble."

Shockingly no one says a word, the males behaved as they always did when together with their constant teasing and play wrestling. I am slightly nervous as to how the females will react when they spot the tree in the field though.

Kira was the first to stop in her tracks, her small hand pressed against her chest. Her eyes wide as she looked around the field. Brittany picks up Keida as the little one squeals in delight at the sight in front of her. RaZ grabs Katherine flying her around the tree so that they can see it from every angle. I see Danny who has been walking quietly next to Victoria take her hand gently in his. She stops for a moment to bend over. She kisses him on the forehead as she runs a loving hand through his hair.

I see every emotion, delight, joy, excitement, wonder, and even a few happy tears. The males all seem to be as mesmerized as the females all except, DaR. He only has eyes for Kira as he watches her intently to see what her reaction is to all this. He must have been pleased, because just as I was going to give the clue for Mossycup to light up. He puts a halt to the proceedings.

"Boys, I need you all to gather around for a moment and then we will let SAGE do her thing." He bends down on one knee in front of Kira… taking her small hand in his gently.

"Kira, I was a male walking through the universe lost and searching until you were placed into my arms. The happiness and the family you have blessed me with there are no words for. I'm afraid I have let you down when it comes to the things that meant so much to you before you were mine.

"I intend to fix one of those mistakes today. Kira, you are the mate of my heart, the very reason for my next breath. I realize that in your previous world there were gifts given to show the world that you belong to another. Forgive me for this being late. I bestow upon you this ring, a gift of my devotion, and a symbol to the universe of my unconditional love. This is my promise to you, until the Lord of Light takes me from this world. Will you allow me to slide the ring I had made for you upon your slender finger as a token of the past, present, and our future?"

"Oh, DaR…how I love you so! Yes, my big growly alien, I accept with a full heart."

DaR rises above her as he gently slides the ring on her finger. And there wasn't a dry eye in the place as he pulls her close, kissing her gently. He leans back, taking his hand wiping the tears from her face. "SAGE, do your thing."

I send the signal for Mossycup to light up and the fireworks begin. The tree starts lighting up slowly first in red, white, and blue pulsing stars. As she became completely illuminated, the stars blink faster as the fireworks boom in the dark canopy, I had created above us, so they could be seen better. The skyline starts to quiet down as the top of Mossycup turns a bright red. The rest of her takes on what looks like long silver streaks racing up and down her frame. Then slowly the red ball starts to lower down as I place large numbers above her. By the time we reach zero the red had fallen to the ground, and she sparkled all over as confetti exploded out of the top of her huge form falling on everyone below.

They all cheer and clap their hands, when she abruptly turns dark again, the whole area around us goes silent as a light fog rolls out from under her massive limbs. Slowly, dark purple and orange lights start to appear as little hologram ghosts float around her in circles. Small orange pumpkins with silly faces pulse upon the ground at her base. Then the grand finale starts as I mimic the Earth's fireworks exploding all above them.

The girls jump up and down cheering as their favorite holidays are being projected in front of them. The guys clap and whistle just as awed by the show as the females are. I couldn't be happier with the outcome so far.

When the field once again becomes quiet. I light up a huge single star in the sky directly above Mossycup. This is her cue to give it all she has. Her massive frame twinkles with small lights at first then with a bright flash she turns into multiple colors all over. Gifts appear upon her lower limbs as the tree dances with colors. Hundreds of small globes appear on the tree with pictures of the boys as they were all growing up. Popcorn tensile wraps the tree as multiple ornaments start appearing all over her. As all of this is going on, I have the bots bring out the buffet I had provided for all of them.

"The show will continue on if you all would like to take your seats. The bots will be around each table with all of your preferred meals."

Keida had taken Kira's hand shortly after they had finished eating and was pulling her around the base of the tree. "Mamma, did you really have all these beautiful things on your planet?"

"Not exactly in this way honey, but yes, we did. SAGE has outdone herself in the preparation of this."

"Did you have a favorite holiday?"

"I loved them all, as it was always a time for hugs and laughter."

"Look at all these presents, this is amazing…I think this one has Danny's name on it. Wait a minute they all have different names on them…can we pass them out?"

"SAGE, can Keida pass these out?"

"Absolutely, I would appreciate her help, but the males can't open theirs yet."

"Danny come here… hurry, help me."

Everyone laughs as the kids run from person to person with a gift in their hand.

"If I could have all the males form a circle. We have a game to play, make sure to bring your gift with you."

It takes a minute to get them to all settle down, but once I was happy with the circle, I announced the rules.

"Now this is how the game will work, I'm going to read you a game from Earth and every time I say the word left you pass your present that way, if I say right, you go the other way. The game is very fast so be prepared."

If their enemies could have only seen them in this form. The males were laughing so hard by the time I finished, they were practically falling on top of each other. After a few minutes, not a single one of them knew their left from their right and they would either drop the present or have several in their hands at once. Once they all settled down. I told them to open the present they had in their hands. I was as excited as they were to see what ANDI had come up with, as their gift.

Each present was unique to the home world of their mother's origination. The males acted like younglings as they tore open wrappers and made a complete mess all around them. I was proud of Keida and Danny as they waited patiently to open their multiple gifts that were still under the tree.

"Hey, all you Unka's get your butts over here. I want to open mine too!"

Lots of apologies followed as they all hurried back to their seats, so they could watch Kira and Danny.

ANDI had done a wonderful job at recreating some of the toys that were enjoyed on Earth. The kids jumped up and down as they tore off the colorful paper. Each toy was ohhh and ahhed over. At one point Tyberius got down on the ground with them explaining or showing them how to use the ones they didn't understand. There were frisbees, marbles, slinkies, yoyos, and even fake swords that lit up when hit together.

After all the males and the children calmed down it was time to give the females their presents. ANDI and I discussed multiple options but finally decided on a gift that represented their past. But first, it was going to be our big reveal.

"Everyone, if I could get all of you to focus your attention over here. SCOUT, ANDI, and I would love to share with you a new advancement of ours, and then we will hand out the last of the presents. I hope everyone has enjoyed this celebration we have put together as we were trying to find a way to merge all of our cultures into one. Everyone, please give a hand to Mossycup for her beauty and for being our model for this celebration. Yells and the males stomping their feet have her bowing slightly.

I take a moment. "Gentlemen I'm ready when you are." The first to pop up is ANDI, he is dressed in a grey suit, with a large top hat, and sunglasses. He bows to the females as he turns around in a circle with his arms out showing off his, sleek yet sexy form.

SCOUT follows behind him in a very intimidating military form. He removes the helmet he had on only to reveal shockingly very humanistic features. Short dark hair lay upon a very hand-some but stern face very similar to Dars. He has pushed the digital avatar to max height as his now tall frame is covered in elaborately heavy-looking armor. His muscles pulse with every move he makes as he turns around showing everyone what a nice firm ass he has.

Damn, I should have known he would pick something straight out of one of my fantasies. The boys start banging their hands on the table screaming SAGE. SAGE.SAGE... I smile for the first time at their enthusiasm at seeing me. It was a last-minute decision to take this form, but as I looked through all the photos available to me. I simply kept coming back to the same ones, my own familiars.

I wore one of Victoria's classy dresses, with the front slightly shorter than the back showing off Alana's long legs, and toned body. I mimic Victoria's perfect posture, as I turn in circles for all to see me. Kira's long pale brown hair drapes down my back, as I turn back around to face the females. I see Brittany reach out like she is trying to touch me. As her own face stares back at her, the only change I have made is the shape of her eyes. As those belong to Katherine, bright green eyes look upon my loved ones for the first time. I curtsy to them all awaiting their final approval.

Tyberius stands up laughing as he walks up to ANDI. "Look at you three, I am amazed and honored to be in your presence. Your forms were and are all well put together. ANDI, the fact that you made yourself look like a Vampire cracks me up. I will send you all the book he has copied his form from. SCOUT, your digital avatar is appropriate and shows the dedication you have always had... to keep your family and this planet safe. You put me in mind of a certain master chief in a game that many humans played. Last but not least...look at you Miss SAGE... your beauty takes my very breath away. The fact that you picked our humans shows how much they all mean to you as I can see them all in your features. Now my only question is how versatile are your forms."

SCOUT speaks up, "Master Tyberius, we are available to the same extent as we were before. Now we can simply appear in this form if need be. These forms are experimental at the moment, but we hope to make them solid in the future."

"I think it's marvelous, it's nice to see a face to go with all your voices."

"Now that our reveal is done, Keida could you help me out once more by handing the females the last of the presents."

She runs over and crawls under the tree since their presents were laid back under Mossycup so they wouldn't get smashed. Keida hands the rolls out and stands back with a huge smile on her face.

"Thank you, sweetie, you have been so much help today. Now, ladies, if you would proceed carefully. ANDI has put a lot of work into getting these completed in the short amount of time I gave him. We hope these gifts will be something you treasure always. But we all three understand the mixed emotions that will come with this."

I watch as each one of the girls take the decorative wrap off the roll and then slowly unroll the parchment inside. The second the roll is opened the paper snaps straight. I watch Kira the closest as she pushes her fist against her mouth the moment, she realizes what she is seeing. Tears flow down her face as she traces the names on the document. ANDI made a huge family tree for each of the females tracing their ancestors from the beginning of public records until the time of the earth's collapse.

DaR steps forward, concern on his face when he sees the tears in her eyes. "Kira?"

"Oh, DaR...SAGE, ANDI, SCOUT... I can't thank you all enough for this. I can't imagine the time or the amount of work it took to put not only these wonderful gifts together but this entire day. I know I will cherish this moment always."

Brittany waves towards XuL for him to join her. "XuL honey, come here and look, my mom finally got away from my ass hole of a father and I had a sister. Thank you, guys, so much, there are no words to express my gratitude."

SoL walks over lifting Alana onto his lap as they look over her family history together. Her hands are shaking as she traces her parents' names. SoL nods his approval towards SCOUT and my own digital heart fills full of the love I could finally see in front of me.

"This is a day. I want all of you to mark your planners. A day for family and loved ones no matter the culture or world they are from. Because it's officially… A House of DaR day of Celebration! Please enjoy the rest of this rising together as Mossycup will continue to show off some of her own designs."

CHAPTER 12

S iN

I can't believe they haven't felt my anger as I feel like I'm ready to boil over at any moment. My so-called brothers are all laughing, teasing, and mock fighting together. Completely comfortable with each other and I hate each and every one of them for it.

I stand here alone, watching! An outcast, that was never claimed, nor wanted. All I want to do is make them feel the same pain that I have had to endure my whole existence.

A movement beside me startles me out of my own mind and back to my surroundings. The most beautiful creature I have ever seen floats effortlessly next to me, but instead of her pulling the shadows into herself to hide her form. She pushes them out and away from her. Making herself glow an eerie white instead.

"Do you plan on standing here forever looking upon the one thing you want the most?"

"I want nothing they have to offer! How do you see me as I am now?"

"You are not the only one cursed to remain or to be pulled back into the mist. I am the same as you."

"You lie! What type of sorcery are you performing to pull me out of my shadow form?"

"You are still as dark as your heart. But as I said, we are the one and the same, SiN."

"How do you know my name? Who are you?"

"My name is Ellaria and I have been waiting on you… for a very long time. Don't let your hate fog your mind about the truth of who you are SiN. Because what we believe is not always the truth."

I reach out for her only for my hand to pass through her ghostly form. She glides away from me. I jump down from the wall, chasing after her as she glides effortlessly just out of my grasp pulling us both deeper into the mist.

CHAPTER 13

K ira

THE DAY WAS an emotional rollercoaster for me and the other girls. I hang the large poster-like parchment up on the wall in the bedroom looking over the names once again. I twirl the ring DaR just gave me around and around my finger. The stones in the House of DaR setting never stop twinkling. It's almost like they're alive somehow.

I reach up running my finger along Rick's name and my heart hits my throat as the pain of losing him hits me once again. I bite my tongue as I try to hold the sobs back. My kids' names blur as the last memories I have of them run through my mind.

"Mistress Kira, I apologize that this gift is causing you so much grief. We were torn on what to do with information that ANDI had available about your previous lives."

"Even though it seems to you all that I'm upset, I'm really not in the way you think. I'm a little overwhelmed but I cherish this SAGE so please don't feel bad about my tears. It's just I never got to say goodbye, there was no finalization from one world to another. Even though I have been told it's been hundreds of years, and I have listened to Katherine and Victoria talk about the end of all we knew. It's just stories to me."

A drawer sliding out of the wall startles me. I look inside only to see a small round disk laying at the bottom. "What is this?"

"This is everything I could find out about your children from the time you disappeared. Both of them were very active on what they called social media. I hope seeing their memories of you and their father and their own lives will give you the closure you need. As I was putting this together for you, I could see so much of you in their mannerisms. Master DaR will be a little while as some of the boys are still here. So, you should have some time to yourself before he comes in. If you insert this disk into your viewer, you will be able to flip through it."

I hold the disk in my hand contemplating whether I am strong enough to look upon their faces knowing they are both gone from the world. Finally, I settle back on the bed and pull over my small viewer. I take a deep breath as I slide the disk inside and then smile when Marisa making a funny face is the first one to pop up. I watch her and Cody's life go by one click at a time. I laugh and cry when they post memories of growing up and all of us together. I held my breath when I saw Cody's wedding pictures and his beautiful bride. A woman I never met, but by the time I was through with the pictures I felt like I knew her well. Marisa married her high school sweetheart and even though it seemed like they never had children, their lives were full of adventures.

I watch Cody's daughter take her first step and then it seems like a few pictures later, she was grown and going to the prom. As the pictures and videos go on, I watch them all grow older. One of the last photos is Marisa and Cody standing together over mine and their dad's grave. Both of them had lived full lives and I feel blessed by the smiles I finally get to see.

I shut the viewer off and simply sit here running their images back through my mind slowly. SAGE has no idea how precious this gift is she just gave to me.

"SAGE, thank you. Now… I believe I can truly move on."

"It's been my pleasure, Mistress Kira."

EPILOGUE

DaR

"Well, father I do believe that the AI's outdid themselves this time. Look at those kids out there playing with those swords. I do believe Danny may have a natural stance with his. How old is he again?"

"Son, I believe he is around seven, possibly eight or so. I'm horrible at keeping up with such things. And yes, I agree those three really know how to throw a party. The moment I saw that female guardian in the middle of the yard I was floored with the details and amount of work it took to pull all of this off, and I believe our females enjoyed it immensely. I hate that Tordan missed all of this though, he would have enjoyed it."

"Yes, I do too, and I agree with SAGE this rising will be marked as a day for our family." We stop long enough to watch XuL mock fight little Danny with their fake swords.

"I believe it's time to start that boy's weapons exercises. By his age, I would have already enrolled my own sons in combat training. I would send him off, but I don't believe Keida would stand for it. So, I will take the boy under my wing and teach him myself as I did my oldest three."

"He is still considered to be very young on Earth."

"Good thing he is on Darverius then. There is no such thing as being too young to learn to defend yourself or the ones you love. I will speak to the child and see if this is something he is interested in doing."

"If Danny does this…You better be prepared to train Keida also."

"Humm, I may have to give this further thought. Because of her size, she needs to be taught by one of her own. I may contact Zura and see if she would be willing to transfer here. She is one of the deadliest females on Xulus. Keida could learn much from one of her own."

"Speaking of Keida, here she comes."

"Hi papaw TY, ANDI told me that you helped him with all the cool toys, you did an awesome job."

"Thank you little one, I'm glad you are enjoying them."

"I'll leave you and your Papaw alone, this old man has had too much excitement for one day."

"Old man my ass," I whisper as Keida hugs him bye.

She raises her arms for me to pick her up. Once her arms are wrapped around my neck, she takes her little hand to my cheek and pulls my face right up to hers. I can't help but smile at her innocence.

"Papaw, I have been thinking. I think you should buy me a ring too! I mean you love me as much as Mamaw and her's sure was pretty."

Before I can say a word, Danny beats me to it. The fact that the child spoke at all startles us both and I don't know who was more surprised by his statement.

"Keida, the only ring you will be wearing is mine. Now come on, let's go play."

I lower Keida back down and her feet no more touch the ground when they are racing off together. XuL flips the fake sword around and around in his hand as we watch them sprint around Mossycup, chasing each other.

"I'm not sure how to react to that, dad?"

"Time will tell son, right now all you can do is try to mold him into a male worthy of that statement. I'll see you back at the house."

I look up at Mossycup and then back to the kids, my soul is full of the love and laughter of this day. My heart is filled with the fact that one moment in time made all of this happen.

"SAGE."

"Yes, Master DaR."

"I want to apologize to you for I never properly thanking you for pushing me to get a housemate. I want to rectify that right now, because of that faithful day…look at the blessings the Lord of Light has given to me… to us. I want you to know, I treasure the very moment Kira was put in my arms and I owe it all to you for making it happen. Thank you, SAGE, for I owe a huge part of my own happiness to you."

"It's been a pleasure, Master DaR."

THE END

The Water Skippers series

Water Skippers
(Kyle and Eden)
A Dragonfly's Whisper
(Nora and Roman)
Earth Shadow
(Lorene and Garret) part one
Shadow Reborn
(Garret and Lorene)
Petal
(Randy and Petal)
Miranda and the Dragonfly King
(Miranda and Tagon)

The Playboy and the Waitress

BOOK BANNER

JENNIFER JULIE MILLER
WATER SKIPPERS SERIES
THE PLAYBOY
WATER SKIPPERS
A DRAGONFLY'S WHISPER
EARTH SHADOW
SHADOW REBORN
PETAL
Miranda and Dragonfly King
The Playboy and the Waitress
THE FORGOTTEN SERIES
FORSAKEN
BETRAYED
FORGOTTEN
HOUSE OF DAR SERIES
DaR
SoL
RaZ

BOOK LIST

The Forsaken series

Forsaken

(Lucas and Emma)

Betrayed

(Tavish and Eve)

Forgotten

(Tyberius and Victoria)

Spin off to DaR

Darverius

DaR

(DaR and Kira)

XuL

(XuL and Brittany)

SoL

(SoL and Alana)

RaZ

(RaZ and Katherine)

A House of DaR Celebration

Who is next…?
Tordan

A NOTE FROM THE JENNIFER

Note from the Author:

I hope… I have made you laugh, and possibly… even squeezed a few tears out of ya. Writing has been a lifelong dream for me, and our dreams are the only thing we have to build on!!!

So GO for it!!!!

I'm an avid reader myself. I believe there are Dragons, Unicorns, and multicolored Kitty Cats, because our imaginations are our own uniqueness.

I want to thank my family and friends for all your support.

To my readers, thank you for encouraging me to continue writing even though my worlds are little different.

After all, I'm Appalachian, and I talk Appalachian. Therefore, I write Appalachian. All my books have country girls in them, and we only know how to speak country girl correctly.

Then to the Lord above, whose blessing gave a poor little girl from Ironton a chance to dream!

If you enjoyed this story, or any of my other ones, I ask that you take a few minutes of your time, and leave a review on Amazon, or Goodreads. It really helps new and older authors alike.

If you would like to stay in touch, hear about new releases, give some advice, or just drop a line.

You can find me on Facebook.

Https://facebook.com/JenniferJulieMiller.

On Twitter.

Https://www.twitter.com/jenniferrick

Or email me at:

Jenniferjuliemiller@gmail.com

Follow me on bookbub. **Https://www.bookbub.com/profile/jennifer-julie-miller**

Follow me on Amazon.

Https://amazon.com/author/jjm5325903

And sign up for my email if you want to learn more about Darverius and DaR's twenty-two sons.

Http://eepurl.com/cfrL8X

DAR

Kira

In the blink of an eye, my whole world has collapsed around me. Headed towards my dream vacation I was snatched right out of the air. My husband, the love of my life, was destroyed right in front of my eyes. He fought bravely, trying to protect me from a horror neither one of us could have ever imagined. I find myself standing in the spotlight on a stage. Mutilated and tortured, the blood from my body flowing freely down my legs along with my will to live. Piercing yellow eyes emerge from the darkness, but even the shadows can't hide his imposing form. Gentle, but terrifying arms reach out for me and within their embrace can I find the will to live again?

DaR

I am a bad ass, known throughout the galaxy for my brutality, as a ruthless and feared commander. With that being said, somehow, I still got coerced into purchasing a slave. My eyes fall upon a small female whose very essence and eternal light is leaking out of her onto the floor below her. I watch in awe as she accepts her fate, willing her nightmare to be over. I almost turn away from her and the unnecessary cruelly in this room, but the very thought of her dying on that floor surrounded by the very monsters that have done this to her disgust me. I walk up among the beings surrounding her and pull her from the stage, daring, or should I say hoping they try to do something about it. The moment I put her in my arms, everything changed. The attachments I have avoided my whole life become unavoidable. Will this damaged slave be able to replace the shadows in my life? One thing for sure is that I will destroy the entire universe to keep her safe. No one touches what's MINE!

XUL

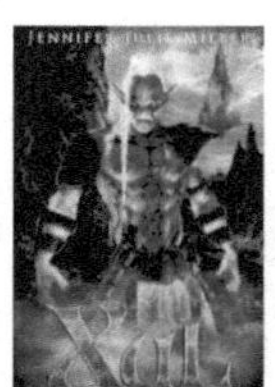

Brittany

All my dreams and wants were stolen from me in the blink of an eye. Awakening, in the middle of a nightmare, I realize I'm being sold like an animal to be studied and dissected in the name of science. Then tragedy strikes, leaving me abandoned and sick. I am only moments from taking my last breath when strong arms pull me from the darkness. I thought it was a blessing that he had found me, the green man who had haunted my dreams. I let myself believe, for just one moment, I might find a small piece of happiness in this unknown world. But what is the old saying? *'Don't count your chickens until they hatch!'*

A blood sucking parasite is eating me alive, literally, and no matter what, I'm not going to survive this horror story. My body is failing me. I beg him to let me go; I just want the pain to stop, but he won't listen. He holds me down and I struggle weakly against his immense strength, choking as blood fills my lungs, when I can't fight any more, Death opens its arms and invites me in.

XuL

My harsh, brutal features have deterred all females no matter the species. I long for companionship and love. Then I find her, my Kismet, the only one made just for me. The one precious thing I would worship above all others. But the fates are cruel especially to a male like me.

I am being forced to destroy the fragile bond that has formed between us, as I have to make the hardest decision of my life. One that will make me lose her either way. I hold her small, struggling body against me, tears flow down my face as she begs me to stop. My heart is crushed as I watch the light leave her beautiful eyes. Upon her final breath, I vow not even Death will keep what's mine.

SOL

Alana

The question is, do I allow this dark moment in time to rob me of the life I could possibly have here? I have never known such horror or fear. If I hadn't experienced it myself, I would have never believed any other living thing could possibly do this to another. The scars may be gone on the outside now, but they will remain forever in my soul. They tell me I can never go back, all that I have ever known is gone. Where does this leave me in the world of monsters? He beckons me, promising me…the fairy-tale… the impossible dream. Everything I have ever wanted to hear! But I don't know if I'm strong enough to go forward as long as the shadows of our past pull me backwards.

SoL

I knew she was withholding the truth from me. I had no idea who I held in my arms, until it was almost too late. The moment her true essence was revealed to me, my body reacted, reaching out for the one thing I had been searching for my whole life… my Inamorata. The very mistress of my heart and now that I have finally found her. I will follow her through the sands of time… no matter how long it takes. I will find my way back to her… because she is MINE!

RAZ

Katherine

How do you go on when all of your wants and dreams have been destroyed? My loved ones were snatched right out of my hands, leaving me alone in a world of unknowns and terror. I'm lost in the in-between with no familiar paths to follow until the sound of a heartbeat and a whisper draws me back to the land of the living.

RaZ

The moment I laid eyes upon her face I knew there would be no distance I wouldn't travel to make her my own. Unknown forces try to steal her from my very arms and even if I have to fight the very essence of her world, the universe, or the very Gods we pray to. Nothing will stop me from making her MINE!

FORSAKEN

<u>Lucas and Emma</u>

Katherine's parents

The one question she often asks herself is *why*. Why has she never been enough? Why doesn't anyone truly want her? She was reminded daily that she was nothing but a worthless girl and only another mouth to feed. The last time she saw her family was the night they dumped her in a ditch on the side of the road and left her to die.

A kind woman took her out of that ditch and gave her a home. Her new family was every girl's dream until a single poisoned scratch took it all away. Emma was tossed away again, becoming a prisoner, and a slave to her circumstances. The one person the Cook enjoyed beating regularly. The day Cook sold her body, all of her hopes and dreams were destroyed. But one fateful night, after fighting for her life, she escapes this, Hell.

He finds her on the brink of death, naked, beaten, and barely alive. She thinks he is the Angel of Death, someone who will save her, but he is a real monster. Did she just trade one Hell for another? Will the memories he steals from her dreams soften his heart enough to make him care for something more than himself? Or will he turn her away, just to *Forsake* her, like all the rest?

BETRAYED

Tavish and Eve

It seems the ones we love the most are the first to Betray us! One such Betrayal cost me everything: my home, my dreams, and almost my life. The second I started running, I knew I would never be who I was or may have wanted to be. All of my choices were taken away with two last breaths, hers and then my own.

The dreams of my youth were destroyed because of the selfishness of others. I fear my life will become nothing but a cold existence of shadows and detachment.

The poison consuming my very soul is nothing but an excuse for me to lash out at the unfairness of it all. It's exactly the justification I need to deliver the pain others have inflicted on me my entire life. Will the emotions of my untried youth destroy my future as I'm forced into a world I truly don't understand?

My own mind has become my worst enemy, and my fragile heart can't withstand another break. I know he's a deceiver, a devil in disguise sent to collect my grieving soul. He is the real monster my mother warned me about under the bed. If I let him, he will destroy me in the end with his mischievous smile and lying angel eyes.

To be loved is the only dream I have left, but we all know Betrayal is the one thing you can always count on to crush you.

FORGOTTEN

Tyberius and Victoria
(DaR's father)

I have known this evil was coming for me my whole life, but that doesn't mean I have looked forward to it! I have run from every sign of the darkness, even to the point of being invisible to the ones around me. I've spent my whole life lurking in the shadows of my family. Keeping myself separate from the ones I love, living my dreams, and wants through their eyes.

I had become so wrapped up in their worlds trying to ensure their happiness, that the day he appeared in front of me. I never once questioned what I was supposed to do. The one thing my family could always count on is that I'm loyal to fault. Even though I made sure never to get too attached because I was terrified the darkness would take them also, it will do anything it can to defeat me. My goal is to survive and to finally see the light.

I have prayed to every God, for this to pass me by, only to know they can't answer. This is my destiny. I will suffer agony unlike anything my mind can imagine, but to be worthy of the light. I need to find a way to face this darkness.

I will never show him an ounce of weakness, but I scream silently for help. I refuse to let him win because he wants me here for eternity. A soul withered in ice, and loneliness, Forgotten in this room of horrors.

All the stars line up for us one time or another. I just have to wait my turn.

THE PLAYBOY AND THE WAITRESS

Jenna

I was always told never to forget that I was worth something too! We all know that every little girl dreams of her knight in shining armor. A man who will ride up and save her from the evil things trying to destroy her. Then, of course, we all know they live happily ever after. My knight was untouchable… A Playboy, a man who stole my heart right out of my chest and with very little effort on his part. Unfortunately, he was also a man whose world I would never fit in. You can take the girl out of the country. You can dress her in nice clothes, have her smile beautifully as you parade her on your arm, but you never really take the country out of the girl. I reach out for the brightest of stars… only for him to leave my heart in pieces crumbling at my feet.

Dage

I watched her for weeks, every smile she bestowed on me captured me in a way no others had. Circumstances throw us together over and over and no matter how many times I hold her in my arms it's never enough. I didn't know what I was missing until she walked away. I know, I can't have them and her...

WATER SKIPPER SERIES

MIRANDA AND THE DRAGONFLY KING

A DRAGONFLY'S WHISPER

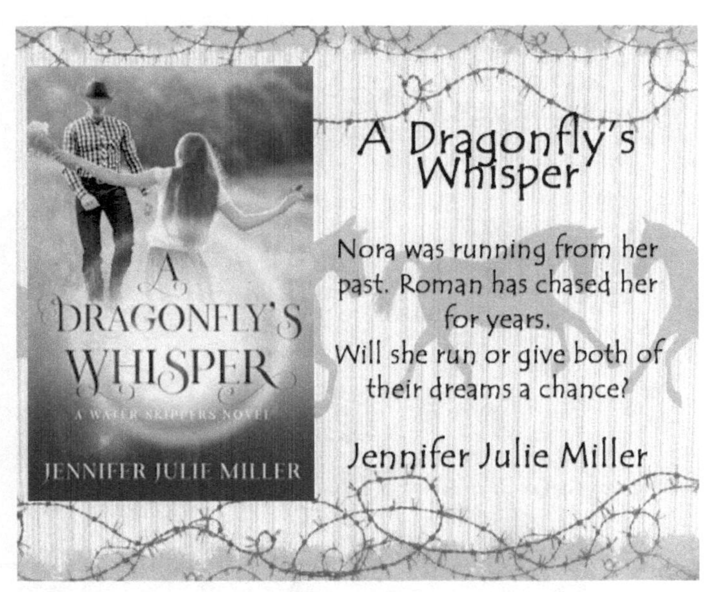

EARTH SHADOW & SHADOW REBORN